WHITNEY HOUSTON

1963-2012

CONTENTS

STAR QUALITY

Supple, soaring and soulful, Whitney Houston's voice carried her to superstardom and provided the uplifting soundtrack for fans around the world

O ver and over again, the pattern was the same: People heard The Voice and were smitten. Whitney Houston, 12, steps out of the church choir for her first solo and blows the roof off. At 15, called onstage by her mom, gospel singer Cissy Houston, she does the same thing—at Carnegie Hall. Months later, Luther Vandross hears The Voice and offers to be her producer. At 19, as she prepares her first album, her mentor, producer Clive Davis, talks in terms that would make a carnival barker blush: "There was Lena Horne," he says. "There is Dionne Warwick. But if the mantle is to pass to somebody . . . who's elegant, who's sensuous, who's innocent, who's got an incredible range of talent . . . it will be Whitney Houston."

Astonishingly, he's right: the world hears The Voice, and—like the congregation at New Hope Baptist Church years before—says hallelujah, making Houston an instant superstar. She will spend the next 29 years living— for better or worse—in the spotlight.

That voice. That smile. And charm. And, let's face it, that body and those legs. Whitney Houston would have been a star in any age, but as the total made-for-MTV package in a world newly gone crazy for music videos, she probably went further, faster than any pop star in history. Her record seven No. 1 hits in a row beat the Beatles; her first album, *Whitney Houston,* became, at the time, the bestselling debut by a female artist.

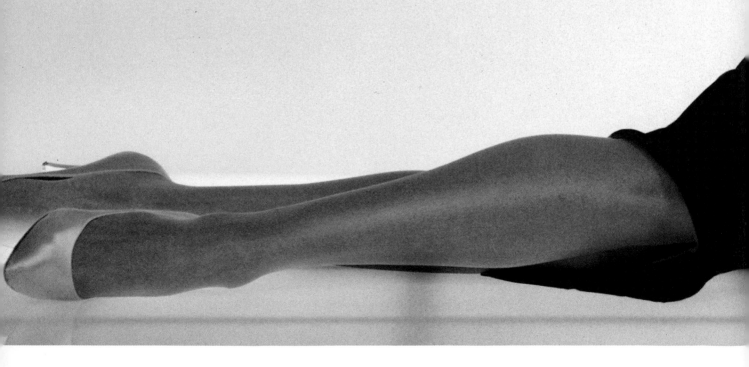

I Wanna Dance with Somebody: The young Houston's light-up-your-life energy (here put in the service of a Coca-Cola commercial) made millions of people, observed a TIME writer, "want to adopt her, escort her or be her."

The pedigree probably helped: Whitney's mom was gospel great Cissy Houston; her first cousin was "Walk On By" singer Dionne Warwick (here with Whitney at a benefit); and her godmother, fondly known as "Aunt Ree," was Goddess of All Things R&B Aretha Franklin.

"She had a model's body," recalls *Essence* editor-at-large Mikki Taylor. "And she loved clothes. Even when she wasn't being photographed, she had her own fearless style. She had a rock-star fabulousness long before they coined that term. In the early days, she loved color— she was utterly fierce with color."

"I'm proud of the way she handles herself," Houston's father, music manager John Russell Houston Jr., said of his suddenly famous, suddenly glamorous little girl (here in 1985). "When she's onstage she belongs to the audience . . . but 15 minutes after she's off, she's my kid again."

After her '80s heyday, the times and styles changed—but Houston (here in 1997), when she put her mind to it, could still play the glam diva.

In 1994, Houston sang at the Concert for a New South Africa, to raise funds for children's charities in the region. Meeting her in Johannesburg, Nelson Mandela said he was there "merely to polish her shoes . . . we love her so much."

Isn't She Lovely: Stevie Wonder and an exuberant Houston at the 1986 American Music Awards in L.A.

A pop culture Mount Rushmore: Elizabeth Taylor, Liza Minnelli, Michael Jackson and Houston at a United Negro College Fund dinner in 1988.

Sean "Diddy" Combs (at the 2010 BET Honors) told Ellen DeGeneres about scoring an invitation to the 1992 Houston-Brown nuptials as an up-and-comer. "It was one of the hottest things in town for the music industry . . . I was like, 'Oh my God! I'm at Whitney Houston's wedding!'"

"Whitney was one of the great vocal athletes of all time," says her voice coach Gary Catona. "And she was one of the most charming people I ever met."

Those close to Houston (here in a 2000 video) said that efforts to market her as an innocent pop princess conflicted with her far grittier, but real, personality. "She was never what you all thought she was," says a relative. "She could swear like a sailor, and they were always worried she was going to drop the F-word in public and it would make people not like her."

After divorcing Bobby Brown in 2007, Houston, making progress in battling a long-term drug habit, worked to launch her career with a new record, *I Look to You*, a tour and glam photo shoots.

Almost from the day her record hit, she was It—
which perhaps surprised her dad, John. When
she was 5 and would sing at the top of her lungs,
Cissy Houston recalled, "her father would say,
'Can't you do something about that girl, about
that screaming?' And I would say, 'Maybe one
day it will develop her voice.'"

SUPERNOVA

Overnight, the shy New Jersey choir girl became
a made-for-MTV sensation, a girl next door with a gloss
of glam, a touch of sass and incomparable pipes

At first she appeared nervous, clasping and unclasping her hands as she sang, her voice a whisper. Whitney Houston was just 19 when Arista Records chief Clive Davis introduced her to the world on the *Merv Griffin Show* in 1983. She performed "Home," a song from the musical *The Wiz*, and, dressed in a puff-sleeved purple top and floor-length black skirt, she looked just like the gospel choir girl that she was. But as the song built to a crescendo, and its singer loosened up, out came that voice—a sound that, in church, could summon angels or shake the rafters—and the world witnessed the birth of a superstar. "You won't forget that name," declared Griffin over the din of the studio applause. "Whitney Houston."

Two years later, that name adorned the cover of Houston's first album, which set sales records for a debut by a female artist. Her second record, *Whitney*, released in 1987, debuted at No. 1 on *Billboard*'s pop music charts. Reagan was in the White House, MTV was in its heyday, and aggressive, political rap was on the rise. Whitney Houston's

Houston as she first enchanted millions. Singer Alicia Keys recalled, as a wide-eyed kid, "watching this beautiful, incredible woman, and [singing] 'I Wanna Dance with Somebody' in the mirror." She was far from alone.

Houston sang backup vocals for Jermaine Jackson in her teens. In 1984 they teamed up for a duet, "Take Good Care of My Heart," a modest hit.

At the height of "I Will Always Love You" fame, Houston met President George H.W. Bush at the White House.

Onstage or in the studio (right), Houston radiated charm. It seemed, said Dionne Warwick, that "her success was something that was supposed to happen."

love-conquers-all pop ballads came as sweet music to the ears of both MTV executives—who were getting heat for underrepresenting black artists—and American pop music fans alike. "How Will I Know," "Saving All My Love for You," "I Wanna Dance with Somebody" and "Greatest Love of All" lit up the airwaves, winning Houston a treasure chest of Grammys and American Music Awards and inspiring a new generation of pop divas. "Here I come with the right skin, the right voice, the right style, the right everything," Houston said later, looking back. "A little girl makes the crossover and VOOOM! It's a little easier for the others."

But those early years weren't always so easy for Houston. At 21, she set out on back-to-back world tours that consumed the best part of four years. And although her family—mom Cissy, cousin Dionne Warwick and her father, John—were a constant support, life on the road proved isolating and lonely for a staggeringly successful and suddenly wealthy young woman who was, in truth, still growing up. "There were times when I cried," she said of this period, "because I didn't understand what was happening to me as a person."

The adoration of her fans was a salve, but criticism—gentle and otherwise—was a constant. Some castigated

Houston for abandoning her roots to appeal to white audiences; though some critics simply surrendered to her overwhelming voice, many sneered that her records were overproduced and—in an era when other artists were busy Feeding the World and Hoping the Russians Loved Their Children Too—too frothy, bland and irrelevant.

It was no secret, to be sure, that the Houston juggernaut was steered by Clive Davis throughout most of her career: He handpicked her songs and teamed her with heavyweight producers and collaborators such as Babyface, L.A. Reid, Jermaine Jackson, Luther Vandross and Stevie Wonder. But Houston's incomparable pipes? Her three-octave range? Only one guy could have produced those. "God gave me a voice to sing with," said Houston. "And when you have that, what other gimmick is there?"

At 24, with a Beatles-beating seven consecutive

Grammys (six in all, including Best Female R&B Vocal in 2000, right) and riches (like Houston's sprawling Mendham Township, N.J., home) came at a price. "When I became 'Whitney Houston' and all this other stuff that happened, my life became the world's," she told Oprah Winfrey. "My privacy. My business. Who I was with . . . I just wanted to be normal."

No. 1 singles under her belt, Houston took a brief hiatus to get her house in order. Or more precisely, the 12,600-sq.-ft. rural Mendham, N.J., mansion she returned to after touring. Her previous home had been a small apartment decorated in shades of lavender, a half-hour drive from where she grew up in East Orange, N.J. So the new spread—with its 25-ft. ceilings and her initials marked in black on the bottom of the pool—took some getting used to. "The bedroom was so large,

sometimes it seemed it was swallowing me up," she later recalled. "I'd sleep in the maid's quarters. People used to laugh at me, but I needed to get a grasp on it. You know, my living space."

Before long, though, Houston had more than just her two cats, Misty Blue and Marilyn, for company. By 1991, she had a new album, *I'm Your Baby Tonight*, and a new boyfriend: comedian Eddie Murphy. "It's not a constant thing," she said. "He wants to know how I'm doing.

Camera-ready, radiant and able to change her look in a flash, Houston was a godsend to MTV—and vice versa.

How I'm feeling. How everything is going. It's that kind of relationship. We're like friends in love."

Houston also made another friend: Boston R&B star Bobby Brown. The pair met at the 1989 Soul Train awards, and she invited him to her 26th-birthday party. A few months later, they saw each other again at the concert of her friends BeBe and CeCe Winans, and he asked her out. "At the time, I was dating someone, but it was kind of *ehhh*," she told *Rolling Stone*. "After a year or so," she added, "I fell in love with Bobby."

The tabloids feasted on the surprising match of pop's squeaky-clean songstress with the Bad Boy of R&B. But as Houston's relationship with Brown developed, her career, at first, continued to soar. Her now-legendary rendition of "The Star Spangled Banner" at the 1991 Super Bowl, later released as a single, is still the only version of the National Anthem ever to have made the Billboard Top 10. But it was Houston's virtuosic rendition of "I Will Always Love

Houston drew inspiration from her godmother, Aretha Franklin (far right, with producer Narada Michael Walden), whose spiritual heir many proclaimed her to be. Eventually a new generation would regard Houston's voice with almost equal awe. "Most women today are simply pretenders to her throne," Luther Vandross once said. "There is only one Whitney."

You," the sweeping ballad she recorded for *The Bodyguard,* her 1992 movie with Kevin Costner, that sealed her reign as the Queen of Pop Divas. Almost inescapable on the airwaves, the single sat at No. 1 on the *Billboard* charts for 14 consecutive weeks—a record at the time—selling more than 8 million copies worldwide. Once again, the fans had spoken. In total, Houston achieved 11 No. 1 hits in her career. But this was, without doubt, her shining moment. And she was just 29 years old.

In the nine years since she stepped onto that studio stage for the *Merv Griffin Show,* Houston had burned brighter than all but a handful of female music stars who had come before. And in spite of the relentless buff-and-polish of the image-making machine that launched her on that trajectory, she had emerged as her own woman: tougher than most knew, a sultry songbird who was, in truth, no longer a choir girl at all. "I am not always in a sequined gown," Houston declared to *Rolling Stone.* "I am nobody's angel."

Poised and ready: Churchgoers knew her as Cissy Houston's daughter, the girl with the marvelous voice and respectful manners who played piano.

GROWING UP

She was a polite child who rarely sought attention—but found it anyway. While still in high school, Houston was working as a fashion model and turning down record contracts

I t seemed like just another Sunday morning in 1975 at the New Hope Baptist Church in Newark, N.J., when a skinny little girl—her friends called her "Nippy"—stood up in her choir robes to sing her first gospel solo. Under the wooden arches that fanned across the ceiling of the beautiful little church, the girl opened her mouth to sing, and what came next, no one who heard it would ever forget.

"Guide me, O thou great Jehovah," she sang, "Pilgrim through this barren land, I am weak, but thou art mighty. Hold me with thy powerful hand."

The congregation, transfixed, stared in wonder. Her father was as amazed as the others. "My wife had told me, 'Your baby is soloing in church for the first time this Sunday. Be there,'" John Houston remembered. "What I heard that day was the voice of a young woman coming from the throat of a 12-year-old child. It blew my mind." Even in a church famous for its choir, little Whitney Houston stood out. "I joined New Hope because the music was the most amazing I had ever heard," says childhood friend Rosanne Martin. "Whitney was in the junior choir. And her voice would light up the church. Her voice had a richness and fullness that could not be mirrored."

The gift was innate. The first time Whitney visited a recording studio, in fact, she was still in the womb—her mother was recording a gospel album—and the girl would be born not long afterward into a family of music royalty. Her first cousin was Dionne ("Walk On By") Warwick; her godmother was Aretha Franklin, known to Houston as Auntie Ree. But it was her mother, gospel star Cissy Houston, who would recognize her baby's talent and would train, discipline and guide her throughout her childhood.

"The soul of who she was, coming of age in Newark, was with her wherever she was in the world," *Essence* editor-at-large Mikki Taylor says of Houston.

By the time of Whitney's birth on Aug. 9, 1963, then-29-year-old Cissy was an established gospel singer and burgeoning pop star. Originally performing with the Drinkard Singers, Cissy and three others formed a backup group, the Sweet Inspirations, who later toured with Aretha, sang backup on Van Morrison's megahit "Brown Eyed Girl" and even performed with Elvis in Las Vegas.

But the bedrock of Cissy's life was the church, and she would raise her daughter with a strong grounding in God and gospel. From toddlerhood on, Whitney tagged along with her mom to the recording studio. "I'd have all kinds of conversations with Aretha and Wilson [Pickett]," Whitney once said. "I just remember being in an atmosphere of total creativity."

Outside church, Whitney was growing up like any Newark kid. She entered first grade at the Franklin School—in 1997 renamed the Whitney E. Houston Academy of Creative and Performing Arts—just blocks from her home on Dodd Street. Henry Hamilton, principal of the school, remembers her well. "She was always very modest, very respectful," he says. "She had great support from her parents, who were lovely. Cissy was involved in PTA activities, Career Day—we'd see her all the time." The youngster was popular with schoolmates. "She would have lots of friends at her house after school, singing," Hamilton says. "Her

brother Gary had the voice. I never thought Whitney would become a singer! But she was the one."

As Houston grew, eventually reaching a willowy 5′7″, she conceived a passion for basketball. "She loved it," remembers childhood friend Liza Donnell, 44, of Newark. "She 'sponsored' our summer league basketball team. She got us together, and we played for her. She wasn't shy. She came to us."

But music remained first and foremost. "I'd hear all this hollerin' and screamin' down in the basement," her father, John, who died in 2003, remembered. "Whitney would be down there with one of Cissy's microphones singing along with Chaka Khan and Aretha records." Auntie Ree was, and remained, her favorite singer. "When I heard Aretha, I could feel her emotional delivery so clearly," Whitney once said. "It came from down deep within. That's what I wanted to do."

In 1978, when Whitney was 15, her mother played Carnegie Hall. "Cissy pulled her up from the audience and said, 'My daughter sings in the church choir, and I want her to sing a song with us today,'" recalls Fern Mallis, a Cissy fan who attended the show. "And she was *extraordinary*! Magical. And she was just a kid! I'll never forget it."

By the late 1970s, Whitney regularly shared the spotlight with her mother at New York clubs. Music critics compared her to Lena Horne; Luther Vandross

Typical teen: Drawn by her look, photographer Bette Marshall shot Houston, 16, at home before she was a star.

Pucker up! "I wasn't surprised she got famous," Liza Donnell, a childhood friend, says of Whitney (in the studio with her mom, Cissy, ca. 1979). "It's in her blood."

The Houston family, ca. 1979: (left to right) brother Michael, Cissy, Whitney, dad John and half brother Gary Garland. "For 40 years," says the Rev. DeForest Soaries, a family friend, "Cissy was managing the life and future of a superstar."

wanted to produce the 15-year-old, but her parents said no. "I wanted her to finish school," said her mother. "I knew if she got started in the business, there would be no stopping her." Whitney, ambitious, rebelled—a little. Reinforcements were called in. "John and Cissy asked me to talk to her," remembers the Rev. DeForest Soaries, a family friend. "Whitney and I sat down at a McDonald's. The disco movement was hot, and she felt her parents were slowing down her emergence as an artist. I said, 'I know it's frustrating, and it may take you a little while to get out there. But no one will be able to ignore you, and no one will be able to forget you.' She just couldn't wait, but she was respectful."

It may have helped that she soon had another outlet for her ambitions. The gangly duckling was maturing into a stylish swan. Just like in the movies, Whitney, 16, was standing with her mother near Carnegie Hall when a scout for a modeling agency spotted her; with startling speed, she began appearing in *Glamour* and *Cosmopolitan*, and, in 1981, on the cover of *Seventeen*. "She was just delightful, a joy to be around," recalls Diane Forden, a *Seventeen* editor at the time. "Just magical. And never, ever a diva."

Heady stuff for a senior at Mount St. Dominic Academy, a parochial school in Caldwell, N.J.

Sometimes Whitney would be absent for weeks, off on location for one modeling job or another. "I had to take schoolwork with me and finish it by the time I got back," Whitney remembered. During that time, she was singing backup for Chaka Khan, Lou Rawls and the Neville Brothers. And word was spreading.

In a 1986 story, *Music Connection* editor Bud Scoppa wrote about what happened next. In 1980 Arista Records' Gerry Griffith went to New York City's Bottom Line club to see flautist Dave Valentin—and came away raving about the opening act, 17-year-old Whitney Houston. Two years later, when Griffith heard Elektra Records was courting her, he pounced. First he went to see her one more time. "I was completely floored," he told Scoppa. "She was mesmerizing. I couldn't believe she had grown so much in that two-year period. She had obvious star quality—it took no genius to see it." He told his boss, Arista's president Clive Davis, and set up a special show for him. "I knew she was good, but she just put on a magnificent performance at the showcase," said Griffith. "The lady's got guts; she's never folded under pressure."

Davis signed her immediately and, for the next two years, carefully created the phenomenon that would burst upon the world.

Houston loved modeling but didn't want it to interfere with her grades, remembers Diane Forden, former fashion editor at *Seventeen*. "She would bring her books to a shoot and sit on the floor, wherever she could, and study," Forden says. "She was that type of person: very dedicated and diligent, whether it was her modeling or schoolwork."

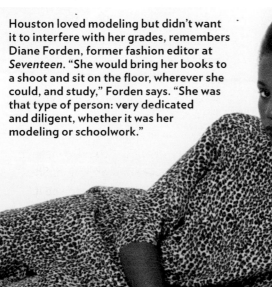

YOUNG AMERICA'S FAVORITE MAGAZINE   NOVEMBER 1981 $1.25

Seventeen

LOOK GREAT THIS WINTER!

- Fabulous party clothes
- Beauty tips
- Outdoor fashions

You can deal with JEALOUSY

60 HOLIDAY GIFTS to make and buy now

QUIZ: Do you really know your best friend?

Super sweater dresses- knit one!

National debut: "There was Lena Horne. There is Dionne Warwick. But if the mantle is to pass to somebody . . . who's elegant, who's sensuous, who's innocent, who's got an incredible range of talent, but guts and soul at the same time, it will be Whitney Houston, in my opinion," music producer Clive Davis told Merv Griffin on April 29, 1983, before the 19-year-old Houston came onstage to make her television debut with "Home" from *The Wiz*. "It's her natural charm. You either got it or you don't have it. She's got it."

Merv Griffin (above, holding hands with the rookie and her mother, Cissy, and below, applauding as Clive Davis and Whitney embrace) was stunned by the teenage Houston's powerhouse performance.

April 10, 1983: Arista's Clive Davis, 19-year-old Houston and the signatures that would launch a career—and sell tens of millions of albums in the U.S. over the next 29 years, according to Nielsen SoundScan.

MOVIES

The music world conquered,
she tried acting—and had
a $400 million hit right out
of the gate

The Bodyguard was a monster hit. Houston's famous recording of "I Will Always Love You" was actually the take done for the cameras, slightly tweaked later in the studio. "She goes through all the emotions of that song as if she's experiencing them," said director Mick Jackson. "You hear her singing that, and you hear the whole movie playing in her voice."

Despite her undisputed status as a pop icon, Whitney Houston was "scared to death," she later admitted to Diane Sawyer, about her film debut in 1992. "It filled her with nervousness: 'How can I do this? Do I take acting lessons?'" recalls Mick Jackson, director of *The Bodyguard*. "In coming to me very humbly, she was showing a vulnerability. This great superstar was actually insecure about some things." Producer Lawrence Kasdan agrees. "There was not an ounce of arrogance about becoming an actress. She knew this was a brand-new step for her."

Houston's fears proved unfounded. While the critical reception was mixed at best—between the MTV Awards and the Razzies, she was nominated for both Best Breakthrough Performance and Worst New Star—the film grossed more than $410 million worldwide, and *The Bodyguard* album, featuring six performances by Houston, remains the bestselling soundtrack of all time.

Twenty years later, Houston's fifth and final movie, *Sparkle,* a remake of the 1976 film about a trio of singing sisters, is scheduled to be released on Aug. 17. *American Idol* alumna Jordin Sparks stars in the title role, and Houston plays her mother. During the six-week shoot in Detroit last fall, she seemed in good health and high spirits. "She showed up either on time or early; she knew her lines," says executive producer Avram "Butch" Kaplan. "She didn't have a personal hair and makeup person; she was so down-to-earth." But what cast and crew remember most is the day in a packed church when Houston sang "His Eye Is on the Sparrow." "Everyone was really emotional. The extras couldn't stay in character. Even the director and producers couldn't keep it together," says stand-in Stefanie Mitchell. "It seemed like a testament to what she had been through, the way she sang that day."

Fans loved the romance, but some critics thought the Houston-Costner matchup lacked chemistry. Said one: "It's like watching two statues attempting to mate."

Brandy (far left, with Houston) played the title role and Houston her Fairy Godmother in *Rodgers and Hammerstein's Cinderella*, a made-for-TV movie that drew 60 million viewers in 1997. "I lost my idol and dear friend," Brandy, 33, said after Houston's death. "Whitney—the greatest voice of all time—you are my angel, and I will always and forever love you."

"She was funny, fun to be around," Penny Marshall, director of the 1996 film *The Preacher's Wife,* said of Houston (with costar Denzel Washington, above and near left). By then, though, Houston was suffering, her drug use escalating. "I would do my work, but after I did my work, for a whole year or two, [I used] every day," she told Oprah in 2009. "I wasn't happy. I was losing myself."

"Whitney and I had this instant connection," costar Lela Rochon (far right) says of 1995's *Waiting to Exhale*. "We had the time of our lives on that movie. It was fun. It was real. It was everything it was supposed to be." A planned sequel, based on Terry McMillan's follow-up novel, is going forward—but no one has been cast in Houston's role yet.

On the last day of the *Sparkle* shoot, Houston "called the cast and crew together and talked about how it was her first film in 15 years, and that they created such a wonderful atmosphere on the set and how she was grateful," producer Curtis Wallace said. "She then asked everyone to join hands in prayer. That is my last memory of Whitney Houston, and it was profound."

"He allowed me to be me," said Houston (clowning with Brown at the 1997 *Cinderella* premiere). "He was fun. Passionate. Loving. It was crazy. We were crazy in love."

LOVE & TROUBLE

No question, Whitney Houston and Bobby Brown had chemistry. Unfortunately, it was the kind that often led to explosions

The occasion was the 1989 Soul Train Awards in Los Angeles. Whitney Houston, repeatedly getting up from her seat to hug friends, kept bumping the head of the guy in the row in front of hers. It was Bobby Brown—there to perform his hit "My Prerogative"—and the two talked. She was knocked out by his dancing ("He was fly—he could move, man," she told Oprah years later), liked what she saw, and, when he asked her out a few months later, was very happy to say yes.

She was America's Pop Princess, Brown the raunchy R&B bad boy, raised in a tough part of Boston, who had been arrested and charged with indecency for simulating sex onstage. Nonetheless, they shared what Houston later described as a "crazy love." They married three years later, on July 18, 1992, in a lavish ceremony at Houston's New Jersey estate. The festivities, for 800 guests, reportedly cost millions; the pair honeymooned along the French Riviera on a $10,000-a-day yacht. The good times continued in November of 1992 with the release of *The Bodyguard*. The movie made $400 million, the soundtrack became the bestselling of all time, and the film's signature tune, "I Will Always Love You," was No. 1 for 14 weeks. Whatever Houston had been before, she could now look down on it from a perch in the celebrity stratosphere.

In 1993, the couple had a daughter, Bobbi Kristina. A year later, Houston won three more Grammys, and *Forbes* estimated she'd earned $33 million in 1994. The world seemed bright.

But only briefly: Increasingly, Brown's wild side began to make headlines. In April 1995, he was charged with aggravated battery and disorderly conduct after a fight at a Walt Disney World nightclub. (Charges were eventually dropped.) That August, he was charged with kicking a security guard during a party he was hosting in West Hollywood. In September, he was nearly killed in Roxbury, Mass., when a fusillade of bullets cut down his younger sister's fiancé as they were leaving a local bar.

Visions in white at their 1992 wedding (her Mark Bouwer gown cost $40,000), the couple looked like they belonged atop their 10-ft.-tall wedding cake.

Houston doted on Bobbi Kristina (in 1998), whom she once jokingly described as "a little diva in training."

Houston later said that, among other things, Brown had trouble dealing with her success, especially as his career began to flag. "I tried to play, 'I'm Mrs. Brown, everybody. Don't call me Ms. Houston,'" she later told Winfrey. "He never liked the fact that people would say, 'You're jealous of her. You're just jealous of her fame and her fortune and what she has.' He would get really pissed off."

Houston, meanwhile, began having her own problems, ticking off her fans by arriving late or not at all. Scheduled as the featured performer for a White House dinner honoring South African President Nelson Mandela, she kept the crowd of 200 dignitaries waiting for two hours. "I just got off tour," she explained, even though she'd played her final date four days earlier.

While the public seemed eager to blame Brown for Houston's changing behavior, some say it was a different story behind the scenes. According to a close friend of the Houston family, "People think that Bobby introduced her to drugs. That's not true. She introduced Bobby to real drugs. Whitney was never a saint. Her public persona was very different from her private life. She was into coke at an early age. It was her escape from this lifestyle that had been created for her."

Houston showed off Bobbi Kristina at a 1993 concert, an era she described as "a whirlwind. . . . I had my baby in my hands, and I had the man of my life that I loved so very much, who I was crazy for, with me."

"She knows the truth," Houston once said of Bobbi, now 18. "She knows what happens in this household."

A couple of glam gals out on the town, Houston and Bobbi attended Clive Davis's 2011 pre-Grammy party.

Numerous friends say that the goody-two-shoes image of Houston was a fiction, created and cultivated to sell albums. Her record company "really whitewashed her," says the family friend. "[They] had to make her appeal to America, the 'I Wanna Dance with Somebody' Whitney. Nonthreatening, perfect angel Whitney. And that was just not who she was at her core. The drugs were her escape from that cookie-cutter lifestyle that she lived on the outside."

The couple's troubles continued. Bobby went into rehab at the Betty Ford Center in 1995, and two years later the couple briefly separated following rumors he was seeing other women. They reunited, but by that time Houston was dealing with a serious drug problem. In a now infamous 2002 interview with Houston, Diane Sawyer revealed that Whitney's mother, Cissy, staged an unsuccessful intervention in 1999 after reports that Whitney and Brown had a fight in a hotel room. "She's old-school," says a relative. "She

never understood the whole addiction thing. She was really supportive of Whitney, or tried to be, but didn't completely understand it. Whitney kept falling into the same patterns. We would all beg her to get clean, and she never would." Over the years, says the relative, the family tried repeatedly, and passionately, to help, to no avail.

In March 2000, not long after winning her sixth Grammy, Houston failed to appear at the Rock and Roll Hall of Fame ceremony in New York City, where she was to serenade inductee Clive Davis, the legendary producer who had launched her career. Three weeks later, scheduled to perform at the Academy Awards with Garth Brooks, Ray Charles and her cousin Dionne Warwick, Houston was fired two days before the show. The official word was that she'd gotten sick. The unofficial word? She forgot the lyrics to "Over the Rainbow" and could barely sing. Said the show's music director Burt Bacharach: "Whitney's chronic condition is very sad."

It got worse; performing at a 2001 tribute to Michael Jackson, she looked like a skeleton in heels. That led to the Diane Sawyer interview, where Houston insisted she was fine and seemed insulted that anyone would believe she did crack cocaine. "Let's get one thing straight," she said. "Crack is cheap. I make too much money to ever smoke crack. Okay? We don't do crack. Crack is wack."

That said, she admitted she had "hung out with some friends and partied" on the night of the Jackson concert, and that she'd used everything from marijuana to cocaine to pills. She added, however, that her only addiction was "making love" to her husband, Brown—who, the next year, was charged with battery after allegedly hitting Houston in the face at their Alpharetta, Ga., home. (The charges were dropped, with her support. She later told *Redbook,* "I do the hitting; he doesn't.")

Their relationship continued to play out like bad reality TV; so, perhaps inevitably, they took it to the small screen. Bravo's *Being Bobby Brown* premiered in June 2005 to good ratings. Whether it was hearing Houston toss out her pet phrase, "Hell to the no!" or watching the couple spat, dance randomly or discuss

Whether onstage (left, at the 2003 VH1 Divas concert) or in court (above), Houston stood by her man. "People had bets on us," she said, "like were we going to make it six weeks? No? Six months?" The marriage lasted 14 years.

At age 15, Houston had sung backup on "I'm Every Woman" for Chaka Khan's 1978 debut solo album. In 1992, she reprised it for *The Bodyguard* soundtrack. That proved a bigger single than the original, peaking at No. 4 on the Billboard Hot 100 and staying in the top 40 for 19 weeks. As a tribute to Khan (center, at the mic with her protégée), Houston proclaims her name at the end of the song.

"My business is sex, drugs, rock and roll, you know?"
Houston, awkward and defensive, said during
her 2002 interview with Diane Sawyer. "I mean,
my friends, we have a good time."

An enthusiastic Houston greeted her husband after his release from jail, where he'd spent 65 days for a parole violation in 2000. Below: Whitney and her mother, Cissy, attended the 2010 BET Honors.

"When You Believe," a soaring, soulful duet by Mariah Carey and Houston on *The Prince of Egypt* soundtrack, won the 1998 Oscar for Best Original Song. On Feb. 11, Carey tweeted that she was "heartbroken and in tears" over the death of her friend.

Brown (with Houston in Miami in 1993) could be supportive. Houston told Diane Sawyer that while filming *The Bodyguard,* she complained that "'I can't do this.... I'm going to quit today.' He said, 'No way.... If you quit now, you're going to blame me for the rest of your life.'"

Her skin-and-bones appearance at the 2001 Michael Jackson tribute shocked fans. Houston's explanation: "I've always been a thin girl. Whitney is not going to be fat, ever. Okay?"

Houston's rendition of "The Star Spangled Banner" at the 1991 Super Bowl turned the National Anthem into a Top 20 hit. It charted even higher a decade later, after 9/11.

the virtues of colonics, the show had train-wreck appeal. Houston, however, decided she'd had enough and refused to participate in a second season.

Without much to do, the pair would sit around their house, watching television and freebasing cocaine, Whitney told Oprah. The couple's relationship frayed to the point where, Houston would later tell Winfrey, Brown spit on her in front of their daughter, cut the head off a portrait of her and painted evil eyes on their carpets and walls.

Finally, one day in 2006, she told Brown she was going out for groceries and never came back. She flew to Los Angeles and eventually filed for divorce.

The split proved nearly as turbulent as the marriage. Although Brown failed to show up in court when a judge awarded Houston sole custody of Bobbi Kristina, he filed a lawsuit claiming his ex-wife was keeping him from seeing their daughter. The suit was rejected, however, when Brown failed to attend a hearing.

Once they divorced, their relationship seemed to improve. She sang at his mother's funeral in 2011, and less than two weeks before Houston's death, she joined him and their daughter for a dinner in Beverly Hills where they "were friendly and in good spirits," according to one observer. "They were just a family having an early dinner; nothing seemed amiss."

During a 2003 trip to Israel, the couple were baptized in the Jordan River. Houston said she felt Israel was her home.

Whitney & DRUGS

A family member talks bluntly about
the singer's long struggle and how those close
to her tried everything to save her

On how the family dealt with Whitney's problems:

We all loved Whitney, and we wanted to see her happy and healthy. It got really discouraging over the years. We'd think she was getting better, that she was clean and sober—and then it would happen again. I can think of five times, at least, when we thought she was going to die.

When she was in Atlanta, we'd take turns checking on her. It was her mother's idea, because she knew that if she went by, Whitney wouldn't listen. Cissy is old-school. She never understood the whole addiction thing. She would say things like, "If she really wants to get past it, she will." But she was really supportive of Whitney; she would have died herself if it would have saved Whitney's life.

For years, Whitney was a functioning addict. She could be using but could pull herself together to make appearances and perform onstage, and she would be terrific. People had no idea she was using, because she hid it so well. But things got worse and worse. Suddenly she had no idea who she was or who you were, and she became angry and lashed out. She would yell at Bobby, at us, at anyone who told her she needed to get clean.

She could be so sweet when she was in a good mood, but then she would become enraged for really no reason.

The saddest thing I ever saw was when [her daughter] Bobbi was about 11 or 12 years old, and Whitney went off the wagon like she always did. I went over to the house to check on them, because it was my turn, and Bobbi answered the door. I said, "Where's your mom?" She said, "She wasn't feeling well, so I put her to bed." I knew I was going to see something bad when I went upstairs. I knocked on the door and Whitney didn't answer, so I was like, "I'm coming in, so you better be decent." And the room was a disaster, clothes everywhere. A chair had been knocked over, the carpet was stained, dirty dishes on the dresser, full of rotten food. It was the bedroom of a junkie.

On the public vs. private Whitney:

Oh my God. [The people in charge of her career] didn't even want her to swear in public. She was turned into someone she was not. She was never what you all thought she was, even in the '80s. She was never that person. She could swear like a sailor, and they were always worried she was going

Houston in
February 2005.

to drop the F-word in public and it would make people not like her. Before she really got into drugs, she would drink a lot, but in a fun way. She could party. But they were worried that she would be seen as a partyer, so she did most of her partying away from the limelight. She complained that she once said the F-word backstage at an awards show, and Clive [Davis] told her, "Madonna can talk like that. You cannot."

She complained about certain incidents but didn't ever put it in a bigger context, like that she wasn't good enough the way she was, so she had to pretend. She just complained that she had

to talk differently in public. She would put on this accent for a laugh, where she sounded—I'm sorry—she sounded white. And everyone would be like, "Oh, that's public Whitney." And we would all laugh. And we'd be like, "You don't have to talk that way. There aren't no cameras here." She loved us saying she was ghetto. That was like her secret.

The lesson is that drugs can affect anyone. This isn't about airing her dirty laundry. But if the kids out there can see that even the most glamorous woman in the world could have this happen to her, it could happen to them too. I hope kids learn from this.

The singer (shooting a video for "Million Dollar Bill") had high hopes for her 2009 album *I Look to You*. Its failure "bothered her," says a music source. "In the music industry, you're only as good as your last hit, even if you are Whitney Houston."

THE COMEBACK

Newly divorced, Houston longed, and worked, to regain her career. But temptation beckoned, and even she knew the high notes might now be forever out of reach

I t could have been, or perhaps should have been, the ultimate comeback tour for Whitney Houston. She was, allegedly, clean and sober after battling cocaine addiction for years, and she'd finally freed herself from a toxic marriage to singer Bobby Brown. "She seemed like she had a new lease on life," says her friend, songwriter Diane Warren. But when the singer, then 46, hit the road in Australia for her Nothing But Love tour in February 2010, "she struggled," says Andrew McManus, who managed that leg of her tour. "She wasn't stage-ready. She just wasn't good enough to dance and keep up vocally." Tickets sold, but the reviews were scathing, calling her "croaky and disoriented." Houston remained undeterred. "She said, 'I know I'm going out there every night and giving it my all,'" McManus recalls of the singer's response to the criticism. "'If that's not good enough, that's not my problem.'"

Indeed, in the last years of her life, many sources say Houston had been forced to face her shortcomings but was determined to turn things around. After years of drug use—Houston told Oprah Winfrey she did cocaine and regularly smoked marijuana laced with cocaine—"her voice was shot, and that bothered her," says a music industry source. But friends say that recently she was working to get back in form. "She was adamant about making everything perfect," says Harvey Mason Jr., who was producing Houston's latest song, "Celebrate," just weeks before her death. "Certain days she sounded really good and other days, like every singer, were not as good. But one of the things that made her a superstar was her drive and determination."

So she battled the setbacks. Compared to her earlier albums, 2009's *I Look to You* was a failure, and it was clear "her comeback wasn't what it was supposed to be," says one music industry source. "Her voice was ruined, and she had to deal with the pressure of knowing that she'd ruined her gift. It was humiliating to her." Her vocal coach Gary Catona admits that when he was first enlisted to help re-broaden her range, "her voice was in bad shape. It was hoarse. But she wanted to return to her former glory, and she wanted it badly." With continued work, "she was sounding better and better," Catona says.

As she tried to get back on track, Houston continued struggling with her sobriety. "It was a daily battle, and temptations are everywhere," says the family friend. Adds another source close to the singer: "She would lie to herself when she said she was on the road to recovery. That didn't happen." Houston finally entered an outpatient rehab program in 2011 at the urging of her mother, Cissy. "Whitney didn't believe in rehab," says a friend of the Houstons'. Still, "she needed to work," says the family friend, who acknowledges that Houston was motivated by tight finances. "She wanted to prove to the film producers and tour promoters that she was okay. She really tried to kick it."

In the months following her treatment, "she was constantly in communication with her counselors, but at the same time she handled sobriety her own way," says the family friend. She continued drinking alcohol "now and then," a source says, but as of last fall, it seemed as though Houston was together and in control. "She seemed to be working hard and was her usual effervescent self," says the family friend. "She sounded strong and happy." With her daughter Bobbi Kristina by her side, "she was recording again, and her life was back on track," says the music industry source.

Houston even appeared to have come to friendly terms with her ex, Bobby Brown. When Brown's mother passed away in January, Houston flew to Boston to perform at her funeral. "She didn't do it because she had to, but because she wanted to," says the industry source. "That's the kind of person Whitney was. Giving, generous and warm. She would do anything to help friends and family."

In a revealing 2009 Oprah Winfrey interview, Houston confessed she had to "pray away" cravings for cocaine: "Don't think I don't have desires for it," she said.

"Whitney knew that it was a different ball game, and she was comfortable with her status and the legacy she had already left behind," a family friend says of Houston (with Jennifer Hudson at the BET Honors in 2010). "That being said, she always felt she had something to contribute."

Houston (performing on *GMA* in September 2009) "was in pain from all the pressure she was facing," says a music source.

Back on the scene, Houston attended the Keep a Child Alive Black Ball in 2010 with Alicia Keys (left) and Jennifer Hudson.

The singer relied on her longtime producer and mentor Clive Davis for support and even money. "During downtimes, she'd reach out to Clive for help," says a family friend. "She had a lot of ups and downs."

Houston began dating Brandy's brother Ray J, himself an R&B singer, in 2008, when she was 44 and he was 27. "We never really thought about what other people think," he told PEOPLE at the time. "We just went, lived life."

Houston's Australian tour was a disaster for the singer (in Sydney on Feb. 24, 2010). "People were coming to hear the voice they remembered," says tour manager Andrew McManus. "The press slammed her performances."

On Thursday, Feb. 9, Whitney partied at Tru Hollywood nightclub and at one point joined Kelly Price onstage.

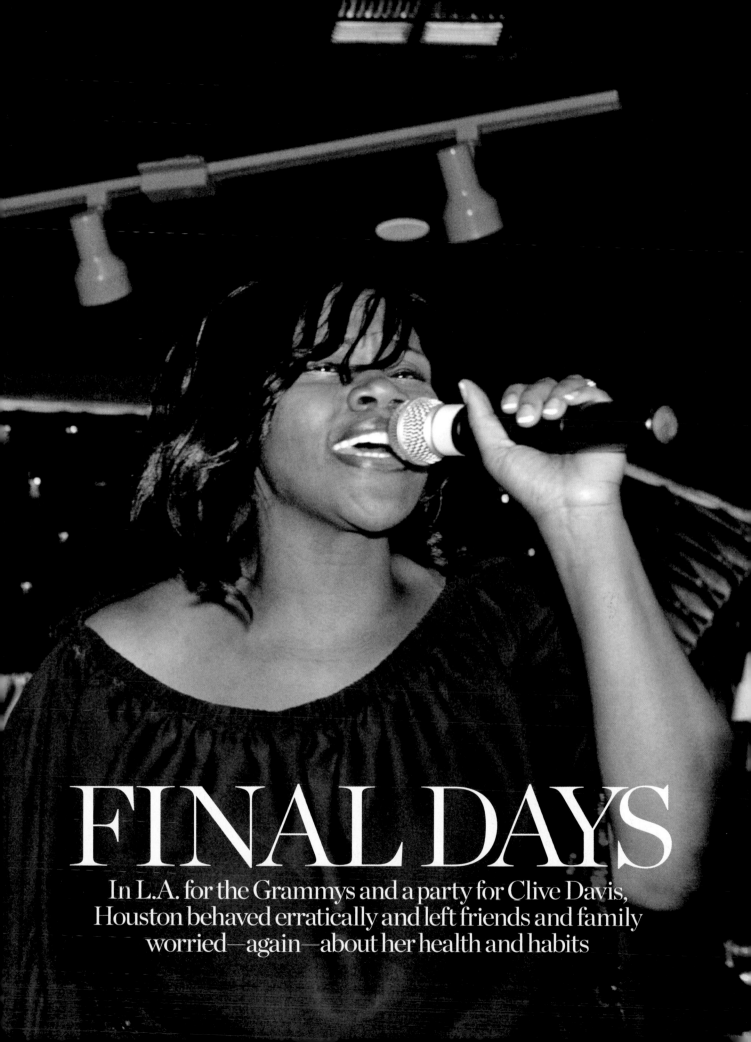

FINAL DAYS

In L.A. for the Grammys and a party for Clive Davis, Houston behaved erratically and left friends and family worried—again—about her health and habits

"Whitney looked very out of it" when she left Tru Hollywood, where the scene was "chaotic," according to a source. "She acted very confused, smiling one second and screaming the next. It was sad to see."

She was, famously, as unpredictable as she was gifted. True to form, without warning during a Feb. 9 party at L.A.'s Tru Hollywood nightclub, Whitney Houston grabbed the mic for an impromptu duet with the night's honoree, Grammy-nominated R&B singer Kelly Price. A sea of cell phones—video apps rolling—swelled around them. "It was like a [rock] concert with lighters in the air," a partygoer recalled. Added another: "The audience melted."

Sadly, it would be Houston's final performance. Less than 48 hours later, a member of her entourage discovered her unconscious in the bathtub of her room in the Beverly Hilton Hotel. After security called 911, EMTs arrived and attempted to revive her, to no avail. At 3:55 p.m., as her brother Gary and sister-in-law Pat looked on, she was pronounced dead. L.A. County Coroner Assistant Chief Ed Winter told reporters authorities had recovered small amounts of prescription drugs in her room, "but nothing alarming." Results of her Feb. 12 autopsy were on hold pending the results of toxicology tests in six to eight weeks.

Since checking herself into rehab last spring for drug and alcohol addictions, Houston, 48, seemed to be "in a better place than she'd been in a long while," said Nikki Haskell, a friend to her longtime mentor, producer Clive Davis. In the hours after her death, stunned friends and relatives struggled to come to grips with her passing, including her mother, Cissy, 78. "She's in disbelief," said a friend. At the hotel, Whitney's only child, Bobbi Kristina, 18, known as "Krissy," her daughter with ex-husband Bobby Brown, wailed, "What's wrong with her? What's wrong with her?" as the paramedics were upstairs. She was later rushed to Cedars-Sinai Medical Center to be treated for stress and returned a day later for more care. "No one," says the Houston friend, "can console her."

After Houston's 2009 comeback album fell flat and her 2010 tour met with poor reviews, the six-time Grammy winner seemed to be getting her once glittering film and music careers back on track. "This was going to be her year," said the friend. But trouble seldom stayed away for long: Last October, a month before she wrapped *Sparkle*, members of her management team tried to convince her to return to rehab, but Houston

"She couldn't handle what happened to her voice," said a source of Houston (leaving a doctor's office Feb. 2). "It crippled her inside."

wouldn't go. "She handled her sobriety her own way," said the friend. In recent weeks, another source says, she'd taken to asking people for small sums of money, saying "she didn't have access to cash" amid rumors Davis was paying her bills but not giving her pocket money. Insiders said Houston, who recently narrowly escaped foreclosure on two of her homes, may have fallen on hard times after supporting loved ones for years. "It was crazy how much money she would pay out," said a relative of Bobby Brown's. "People just took and took from her."

In the days leading up to the Grammys, Houston's behavior was erratic. Recording a new song for the *Sparkle* soundtrack in L.A. Feb. 7, "she got in the booth and worked hard for about three or four hours," says producer Harvey Mason Jr. "She was having fun and acted normal." But the next day, said a witness at the Beverly Hilton Hotel, Houston "was out of it," slurring and cursing as she spotted a headline on a tabloid that said she'd collapsed. In the early hours of Feb. 10, leaving Tru Hollywood, she bore small cuts on her legs and "looked disheveled and stressed," a source says; afterward, while partying at the club Playhouse, "she seemed completely out of it," said a witness.

The strange behavior continued on the eve of her death, when, after a swim in the hotel pool, "she was a complete mess," a source said. Adds another: "She twitched her nose constantly."

In the hours after her death, celebrity guests began to arrive at the hotel for Davis's annual pre-Grammy soiree, which Houston had looked forward to attending. Showing up after many of his guests had arrived, Davis took the podium looking visibly distraught. "I do have a very heavy heart," he said.

On Feb. 13, Houston's body was flown back to New Jersey and taken in a gold hearse to a funeral home in Newark. A funeral was planned for Feb. 18 at New Hope Baptist Church, where she'd sung as a child. Despite the tragic way she died, those closest to her say she'll be remembered as much for her inimitable gift and a kind heart. "She would do anything for those she loved," her friend says. "And she was one of the greatest voices of her lifetime."

"Clive is just overwhelmed with this," said Nikki Haskell, a friend of Davis (with Alicia Keys after the news broke).

Nine hours after the 911 call, Houston's body was taken from the Beverly Hilton to the morgue.

After Houston was pronounced dead in Room 434, hotel security was tight—even her famous cousin Dionne Warwick wasn't allowed upstairs.

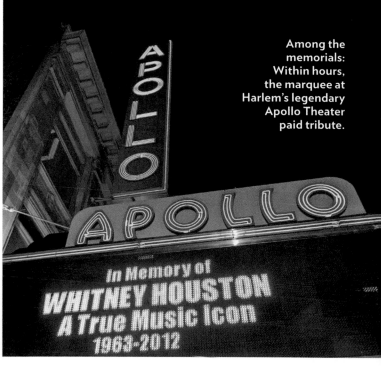

Among the memorials: Within hours, the marquee at Harlem's legendary Apollo Theater paid tribute.

In Memory of
WHITNEY HOUSTON
A True Music Icon
1963-2012

Remembering WHITNEY

FRIENDS REMEMBER

"To me Whitney was THE VOICE. We got to hear a part of God every time she sang" —OPRAH WINFREY

"When I started my English career, I wanted to be like her. I loved her so much" —CELINE DION

"My favorite female singer. The best voice—the most natural, sexy-sounding person that I have ever heard" —SIR TOM JONES

"It was the greatest honor of my life to be able to be the one to pay tribute to Whitney's memory [at the Grammys]. I haven't stopped crying since she passed. Her family is in my prayers" —JENNIFER HUDSON

"I was brought to tears again last night, as I'm sure many were, when Jennifer Hudson sang 'I Will Always Love You' at the Grammys. . . . I am still in shock. . . . We will always love you" –DOLLY PARTON

"She will be remembered as one of the greats who changed music. Everyone will suspect certain things, obviously. But the truth of the matter is that what it really is is unbelievably sad" –GEORGE CLOONEY

"She was a she-ro to millions of women. She was an absolute pioneer. One of the greatest voices on the planet" –WYNONNA JUDD

"She was the Grammy queen. I had so many Grammy moments just watching her, being at home and being inspired and wanting to be her" –FERGIE

FAREWELL

"Whitney had phenomenal success overnight, and perhaps too much too soon.... Let us all applaud and remember Whitney for the beautiful, giving and caring young lady and talented artist that she was, the great music and performances. Remember the hits. Forget the misses. A true superstar has gone on...." —ARETHA FRANKLIN

MASTHEAD

Editor Cutler Durkee **Design Director** Andrea Dunham **Photo Director** Chris Dougherty **Photo Editors** C. Tiffany Lee-Ramos, Florence Nash **Art Director** Cynthia Rhett **Designer** Joan Dorney **Writers** Steve Dougherty, Kristen Mascia, Anne-Marie O'Neill, Sarah Saffian, Jim Seymore, Craig Tomashoff, Charlotte Triggs **Reporters** Ellen Shapiro, Debra Lewis-Boothman, Sabrina Ford, Mary Hart **Copy Editors** (Chief) Joanann Scali, (Deputy) James Bradley, (Coordinator) Aura Davies, Ellen Adamson, Jennifer Broughel, Pearl Chen, Gabrielle Danchick, Valerie Georgoulakos, Lance Kaplan, Alan Levine, Jennifer Shotz **Scanners** Brien Foy, Salvador Lopez, Stephen Pabarue **Group Imaging Director** Francis Fitzgerald **Imaging Manager** Rob Roszkowski **Imaging Production Manager** Charles Guardino **Imaging Coordinator** Jeff Ingledue

Special thanks: Céline Wojtala, David Barbee, Jane Bealer, Patricia Clark, Margery Frohlinger, Suzy Im, Ean Sheehy, Patrick Yang

TIME HOME ENTERTAINMENT

Publisher Richard Fraiman **Vice President, Business Development & Strategy** Steven Sandonato **Executive Director, Marketing Services** Carol Pittard **Executive Director, Retail & Special Sales** Tom Mifsud **Director, Bookazine Development & Marketing** Laura Adam **Publishing Director** Joy Butts **Finance Director** Glenn Buonocore **Assistant General Counsel** Helen Wan **Assistant Director, Special Sales** Ilene Schreider **Book Production Manager** Susan Chodakiewicz **Design & Prepress Manager** Anne-Michelle Gallero **Brand Manager** Michela Wilde **Editorial Director** Stephen Koepp

Special thanks: Christine Austin, Jeremy Biloon, Jim Childs, Rose Cirrincione, Lauren Hall Clark, Jacqueline Fitzgerald, Christine Font, Jenna Goldberg, Hillary Hirsch, Suzanne Janso, Amy Mangus, Robert Marasco, Kimberly Marshall, Amy Migliaccio, Nina Mistry, Dave Rozzelle, Adriana Tierno, Alex Voznesenskiy, Vanessa Wu

FRONT COVER
Lance Staedler/Corbis

TITLE PAGE
Sante D'Orazio/Corbis

CONTENTS
Randee St. Nicholas/Contour by Getty Images

STAR QUALITY
4 Mark J. Terrill/AP; **6** Dirck Halstead/TLP/Getty Images; **8-9** Diana Lyn/Shooting Star(5); **10** Everett; **12** Lance Staedler/Corbis; **14** Richard Corman/Corbis; **15** Firooz Zahedi/Trunk Archive; **16** (from top) Juda Ngwenya/Landov; Ron Galella/Wireimage; **17** (from top) Richard Corkery/The NY Daily News/Getty Images; Brad Barket/PictureGroup; **18** Randee St. Nicholas/Contour by Getty Images; **20** Wenn; **22** Randee St. Nicholas/Contour by Getty Images

SUPERNOVA
24 Steve Prezant/Corbis; **26** Globe; **27** (from top) Dave Hogan/Getty Images; Jerome Delay/AFP/Getty Images; **28-29** Dirck Halstead/TLP/Getty Images(2); **30** Ramey; **31** Vince Bucci/AFP/

Getty Images; **32** Diana Lyn/Shooting Star; **33** Peter Mazel/Sunshine/Zuma; **34** John Gladwin/PA/Landov; **35** Everett

GROWING UP
36 Sam Emerson/Polaris; **38** Rex USA; **39-42** Bette Marshall/Getty Images(3); **43** (clockwise from top left) Carmen Schiavone/Seventeen Magazine; Bette Marshall/Getty Images; Seventeen Magazine; Doug Vann/Corbis; **44-45** Christina Thompson/Contact Press Images(3); **46** Ebet Roberts/Redferns/Getty Images

MOVIES
48 Photofest; **49** Warner Bros; **50-53** Photofest(4); **54** Alicia Gbur/Sony

LOVE & TROUBLE
56 Andrea Renault/Globe; **59** Gilbert Flores/Celebrity Photo; **60** Eugene Adebari/Rex USA; **61** (from left) Tibrina Hobson/Wireimage; Jen Lowery/Splash News; **62** Joe Cavaretta/AP; **63** Erik S. Lesser/AP; **64** Randee St. Nicholas/Contour by Getty Images; **66** Ida Mae Astute/ABC/Getty Images; **67** (from top) Jon James/

LFI; Frank Micelotta/PictureGroup; **68** Anita Weber/Capital Pictures/AdMedia; **70** Cesar Vera/Contour by Getty Images; **71** (from left) Beth A. Keiser/Reuters; George Rose/Getty Images; **72** Eliot Press/Bauer-Griffin; **74** INF

THE COMEBACK
76 Frank Micelotta/PictureGroup; **78** George Burns/Harpo Productions; **80** Frank Micelotta/PictureGroup; **82** Derek Storm/Retna; **83** Kevin Mazur/Getty Images; **84** (from top) Mario Anzuoni/Reuters; Denise Truscello/Wireimage; **85** Don Arnold/Wireimage

FINAL DAYS
86 Gabriel Olsen/Filmmagic; **88** David Tonnessen-Ben Dome/Pacific Coast News; **89** FameFlynet; **90-91** (clockwise from top left) Mavrix; Pacific Coast News; Dave Kotinsky/Getty Images; Ben Dome/Pacific Coast News; **92** Robert Gauthier/LA Times/Polaris; **94** Mario Anzuoni/Reuters; **96** Neil Matthews/Retna

BACK COVER
Patrick Demarchelier/RCA

ISBN 10: 1-61893-004-4, ISBN 13: 978-1-61893-004-0, Library of Congress Control Number: 2012933290